good for one day of

help aro

hou

cooking raking butter-churning
scrubbing sweeping sewing
mopping ironing washing etc.

for

the world's greatest mom

from

place this card outside your door for

breakfast in bed

eggs:

- fried
- scrambled
- poached
- omelette

sides:

- cereal
- bacon
- sausage
- potatoes

starches:

- toast
- pancakes
- waffles
- french toast

drinks:

- coffee
- tea
- o. j.
- ice water

for

the world's greatest mom

from

redeem this card for a
day of pampering
at:

for

the world's greatest mom

from

for

the world's greatest mom

from

redeem this card for

a restoring

hike

for

the world's greatest mom

from

redeem for a day of

beauty

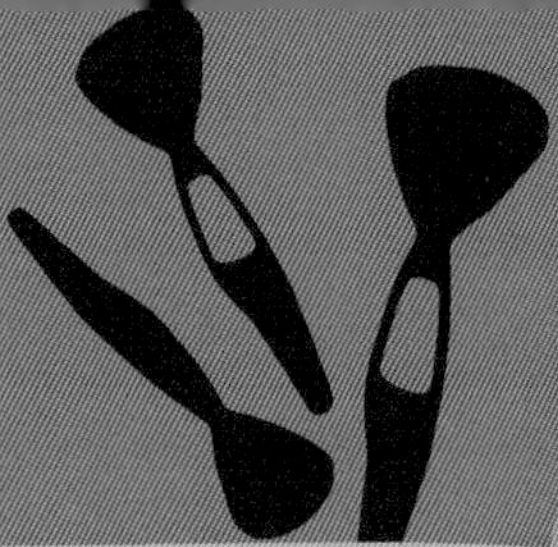

nails:

hair:

makeup:

for

the world's greatest mom

from

this card entitles you to
at chez nous

for

the world's greatest mom

from

this card entitles the holder to
a day at the
beach

for

the world's greatest mom

from

this card is good
for one free

for

the world's greatest mom

from

redeem for
one full week of daily
super-duper
extra-
thorough

dish duty

mon tues wed thurs fri sat sun

for

the world's greatest mom

from

use this card
for a
picnic
in the
park

for

the world's greatest mom

from

bath/shower

toilet

this card entitles you to

a sparkling-clean bathroom

floor

sink

for

the world's greatest mom

from

redeem this card for
one week's personal

caffeine delivery

service

your order:

for

the world's greatest mom

from

redeem this card for

one night free
of all mom responsibilities

out on the town ★ ★ in on the couch

for

the world's greatest mom

from

this card entitles the holder

to one **absolute** and **unconditional** **yes**

for

the world's greatest mom

from

use this card for

for

the world's greatest mom

from

this card entitles the holder to

tickets to

for

the world's greatest mom

from

this card entitles you to a day of complimentary, full-service

laundry

- wash and fold
- delicates
- dry cleaning

for

the world's greatest mom

from

this card entitles you to your own personal
garden assistant

for

the world's greatest mom

from

redeem this card for three

pick-up and deliveries

of your choosing

one:

two:

three:

for

the world's greatest mom

from

this card entitles you to

a very special

weekend getaway

to: ____________________